Betting on One Percent
"Every Roll of the Dice is Golden!"

Sabrina K. Carpenter

Betting on One Percent
Copyright © 2010 by Sabrina K. Carpenter

All rights reserved. No part of this book may be reproduced or transmitted in any form or by any means without written permission from the author.

ISBN # 9780982773703

Published in the USA by Perfected Pen Publishing. (www.PerfectedPenPublishing.com)

Dedication

I would like to dedicate this book to all those who continue to defy the odds. My bet is on you!

To Michelle Nunn, my 8th grade English teacher, who saw my talent immediately and dedicated herself to nurturing my love for words. Wherever you are, I hope you know how appreciated your efforts have been. Your influence will remain with me throughout my life!

Introduction

My nickname is the "One-Percenter". I have spent my entire adult life defying odds. People began realizing that anything with a one-percent or less chance of happening…would happen to me. Thus, the nickname stuck around.

I was diagnosed with cancer at age 19 and endured a 5-year battle with the disease. I was told that I would likely never be able to have children. But, they didn't bet on my odds. I now have two extraordinary boys, Isaiah and Micah, who are daily reminders of my many blessings.

I have established a successful freelance writing business, Perfected Pen, as well as a publishing division, Perfected Pen Publishing. Many people told me that writing wasn't a "real" job. I had a natural gift and with refinement and perseverance over the years, I was able to turn that talent into a career. So, the critics lost that bet.

Writing became an outlet for me at a very early age. Poetry was my first love. Some of my work is inspired by the headlines, some from personal experience and some simply derived from a great imagination.

The writing I compose for businesses is structured and concise, however, my creative writing is poignant and at times, raw. So, be prepared for a ride with the "One-Percenter". It's a journey you will never forget!

~Sabrina K. Carpenter~

Enough is Enough

I pluck IV's from my veins like petals from a rose
Watching the blood trickle down my arm
For that moment alone
I know
I am still alive.
I never chose to be sick.
I never chose to be a statistic.
But sometimes Life has nothing to do with being Pro-Choice.
Dying a bit inside every time they tell me to count down from ten
Knowing I never make it past 8,
Wondering if this time my heart rate
Will cooperate
Through sedation,
With doctors who can't relate
To anything other than arrogance.
When will enough be enough?

Why have incisions turned into painstaking decisions?
White crisp linens becoming my confessional, my mosque, my temple,
Praying to any God who would make these complexities simple,
The stench of stretching latex,
Filling nostrils feverishly searching for air that is pure,
My mind confident but my body unsure
If a cure would come from
Scalpels scarring tissue
Tissue wiping tears
Tears flowing through a Morphine drip
Equipped with false sensations
Erasing lab rat minds filled with trepidations
Enough is enough!
Is it time to wake up?

Class is in Session

Educational lessons,
Within textbooks
Containing blank pages,
I skip stages,
And fly free like a cage-less
Bird.
Lacking the lessons learned
To elevate myself to higher plateaus,
I found myself below
The curve of womanhood.

I deleted "misunderstood"
From my dictionary of excuses,
And analyzed the repercussions that my action produces.
Tired of sitting in life's classes,
Being held back with the masses,
Never learning what differentiates
Who fails from who passes.

Honing in on my inner woman,
I learned now what I should have done then,
I ditched the helpless girl,
And picked up my mighty pen.
Empowering text,
Previously vexed
By my own insecurities,
I chose to challenge instead of appease,
Finding no need
To ever return to the cage,

That enslaved
Me.
But this time,
I fly,
With knowledge on my wings,
Ready for the intense lessons that life brings.
I write my own pages,
As a woman with no cages,
Singing of life's graces,
Living above the curve of womanhood.

"Brave New Voices"

I see myself in you...not just writing for shits and giggles but truly trying to figure out how to transform adversity into success, wondering how you can overcome tribulations that continue to trip you on every step of your journey, and grasping at straws but as a poet you know it's too cliché, so you pray...to your pen and pad.

I see myself in your confusion...young mind creating its own illusions, playing tricks on what should be reality when reality...is merely an illusion, knowing the stage is the only one who can really hear your talent without judgment, you stand and beat her, and every time you meet, you can't defeat her...but she listens to your stories nevertheless.

I see myself in your passion...a young adult trying to drop the "young" when society never listens to the lessons you speak, you pull over on the side of the road and spray your message far larger than the egos that never bother to read them...can you hear me now?

I see myself in you...that light in your eye that doesn't just gleam, it screams, and one day baby girl you will rise above it all and to your own surprise your words will echo in each of our ears and only a select few, who bothered to listen, will recognize your Brave New Voice.

Shelter

Hunger pangs disguise themselves as belly aches,
In goofy glasses and a fake moustache,
Hoping to fool my stomach into believing there would be more to come.

Seeking shelter in the stories Mommy creates.
My babies dodge raindrops like a schoolyard ball,
We hide in shadows where we easily become invisible to the world.

I used to be you, looking down upon me apathetically,
Thinking homelessness wasn't my problem,
Until one day...it was.

Pride gets lodged in my throat like a kerosene-drenched towel,
Igniting my tears when I am forced to ask for help,
But, only few are capable of extinguishing my flames.

Noble gestures of generosity create a puppet show,
Opening up doors previously sealed shut by indifference,
Casting light on our shadows for all the world to see.

My Affair

I find myself drawn to him even while sleeping beside my husband in bed, my fingertips constantly stroking his ego, there is no end in sight.

I have tried to repress the desire, to cut off all ties but he makes me feel invincible every time the two of us combine.

I have been told that he is no good for my soul, a constant battle to keep him at home when he is so obviously in control of so many others.

Caressing curves, creating words that others find obscene, we bask in our love affair.

Public displays of affection create adrenaline rushes, with eyes of voyeurs filling with obsession.

So, I am sorry for those that are hurt by the stories we compose, it has never been our intention,

Just the consequences of, just the repercussions for, My love affair with Poetry.

Harlem Station

I sit in the Harlem train station,
Patient,
Listening to a man gripe
About stereotypes
And the injustice in the world.
I see the genuine pain that is hidden
Behind a façade of apathy he didn't
Intend to be seen.
It's 2am,
And it is just me and him,
Conversing on a whim.
He adjusts his fish nets and I rub my 6-month tummy,
Thinking about what a funny
Sight this must be
For the eyes that just see
A pregnant woman and a transvestite,
Instead of the actuality
Of the situation which is merely 2 human beings
Seeing,
The world through each other's eyes.
The train arrives.
We both return to separate lives,
He adjusts his halter top and I feel my baby kick,
And just as quick
He sashays off and leaves,
As I take a piece of Harlem with me.

The Tat

I forget how open the wound still is,
Etched in his chest like a battle scar,
I never remember the anniversary of the day
That he can't seem to forget.
It was in slow motion,
It was déjà vu to the umpteenth degree.
I never told him I saw his father
Before the ambulance left.
Guess the cat's out of the bag.
I thought burn victims looked like that in horror flicks
Not outside of his home,
Not to the man who raised him,
Not like this.
His focus became overwhelming grief,
Staring at flames he would later etch in his chest,
And I saw myself standing inside, only 11 years prior.
I was prepared to guide him down this charred path,
Days later still digging through memories
Saturated by fire hoses.
But the path led us down the burn unit hallway,
And I wasn't prepared for that.
I wasn't prepared to watch his reaction,
To a reality that haunted my nightmares for years.
To see a man he loved,
Yet with no visible features to decipher him.
To say goodbye, as best he could,
Etching the pain in his chest.

Mail Order Baby

I'm tired of meeting girls longing for a baby to dress up in clothes that the stork brought to Candyland. Motherhood is not a game, nor the land of make-believe and if sleep is still that important, I suggest you hang up the dream.

I wore every pound like a badge of honor, knowing that my reward would be a child that superceded the best of me and if you plan to starve yourself to maintain your figure, save us all the eye rolls and buy yourself a puppy.

There is no room in motherhood for selfishness and if each sentence is centered around "I" or "Me" with no room to include "He", "She" or "We", this job isn't for you!

I'm tired of meeting girls longing for a baby, only to follow the statement with unrealistic pre-cursors while still requiring your own purser to be at your beck and call.

Flipping through pages of eye color and hair, expecting to pick out features from a Sears catalog, I must grab you from out of that fog and explain that as a mother, your child is PERFECT! Period.

I'm tired of meeting girls not ready for the responsibilities of women!

Fine Wine

He said he was not only in love with me...
But also with the person I was destined to be.
Those words blew my mind
Like the atom bomb
Leaving mere remnants of a past that existed before him.
I swirled the words around in my head
Like a fine wine
Allowing the sweet taste of acceptance
To penetrate every crevice in my overactive mind.
Gently spitting the syllables back into my glass
And inhaling the aroma of forever.

The Confession

He spoke of himself in vague terminology and minute gestures, in hopes not to set off any radars.
I knew of the secrets he wanted to scream before he ever whispered a word.
He wanted to replace discretion with profession,
To finally feel free from the stigmas of our society.
But instead, after ending a phone call with "I'll be home soon, baby"
They would look at his left ring finger and ask,
"Oh, the old wife, eh?"
He robotically laughed and replied, "You know how that goes!"
All the while feeling as hypocritical as those he was hiding from.
The 1st time I saw him with his "wife", I was in awe.
She held his hand with such conviction,
Hairy knuckles intertwined,
Laughing as carelessly as children in a schoolyard,
Embracing with inflated pectorals connecting like the perfect puzzle piece.
And SHE finally dropped the "S".
The beauty of that moment…
The beauty of witnessing the weight lifting from his chest,
As he introduced "Thomas" as the love of his life,
Was beyond any sunset,
Surpassed the most boastful Venetian horizon,
And exceeded any connotation of love that I had ever seen.

From that point on, he spoke of himself in specific terms and gestured as grand as the topic allowed,
  And his "wife" proudly became "HE" again,
  Because he rid himself of much more than the "S"
  The day he told me it was time to confess.

Anniversary

3 years ago today
Pews filled with glassy eyes
White lace laying softly against auburn hair
The 2nd hand ticking comically loud as if a reminder
That I was on borrowed time.

3 years ago today
Fingers intertwined
Placing material rings on virtuous vows
Catching tears with mascara covered lashes as if a reminder
That you must learn to fall before you can learn to fly.

3 years ago today
Blessings called forever
Were bestowed upon 2 mortals
Not needing a reminder
That I "do" can become "I will always".

3 years ago today
Minds couldn't fathom the possibilities of the impossible,
Gazing at a mirror image of you
Within the blue ocean eyes of our son
Born miraculously 10 weeks ago today as if a reminder
That our borrowed time has become infinite.

Reading at Sunset

Perhaps my legacy will be invisibility, the ability to have taken up space in a moment of time but never seen taking paces, just miming the actions of the visible.

Perhaps my words will be of the unheard, silenced by deaf ears that fear the sound of prophetic verse coerced by anonymity.

Perhaps my definition will remain undefined, long after the aftermath of Webster's demise.

The Messenger

The details of that day haunt me like the ghost of Christmas past.

I can still feel the texture of her curly Puerto Rican hair between my fingers as I secured her ponytail.

The sound of her squeaky laugh – a mix between Rosie Perez and Elmo,

It was endearing.

I asked her what she wanted to be when she grew up.

"Bri-Bri" she said, "I want to help people get along. What's the name of that job?"

And before I could come up with a creative answer fit for a 7-year old, she concluded,

"Yup, that's what I want to be!"

The day continued,

Birthday cake turned bellyache,

Running in circles,

Occasionally tripping over an unruly shoelace.

And if you think you know what injustice is, try standing 4 feet 3 ¾ inches away from a future luminary in our society as a bullet penetrates in...and then milliseconds later out of her skull,

Directly between her inculpable green eyes as if the work of a militant sniper.

Her blood preceding her fall like a red carpet laid out from Heaven,

The unison of gasps serving as her

Premature version of Taps,

And all I could think is "I never answered her question."

Gunfire continued between the red and blue,

And although insanely oblivious to my surroundings,

I knelt down next to her convulsing body and whispered in her ear,

"A Messenger baby girl, you are our messenger of peace!"

Soul Mate

I've never believed that there is only one love of your life.
I've never believed that you only have one soul mate in this entire world.
My gut feeling was right.
I fall in love all over again...every day!
Every time I look into the blue eyes of my 2 amazing boys...
Every time they learn something new...
Every smile...
Every snuggling moment...
We were meant to share our souls with whoever is willing to accept.
We were meant to love whoever is willing to reciprocate.
And who better than our children?
So, to my soul mates, my true loves, my precious sons,
I look forward to loving you more and more...every day of our lives!

Release Me

Free from your judgments,
Free from the misconceptions,
Free from caring about
Other people's perceptions.
No longer your puppet
To alter and control,
Free from being an alter ego,
Free to be me, free to be whole.

Spent years trying to conform to what you wanted me to be,
Body too thin, too thick,
Too quiet or speak to quick.
Spent years trying to become someone everyone else wanted,
Too smart, wordy, and bright
Too rude or too polite.
Lost my identity by trying to please others,
Too plain, face too made up,
But I became free the day I gave all that up.

Free from your judgments,
Free from the misconceptions,
Free from caring about
Other people's perceptions.
No longer your puppet
To alter and control,
Free from being an alter ego,
Free to be me, free to be whole.

I stripped myself of everything untrue,
Freed myself from the layers of fake,
Eliminated the excess,
And allowed myself to make mistakes.
I bared my soul for the world to see it all,
And although venerable and exposed,
I was free from now being juxtaposed.

Free from your judgments,
Free from the misconceptions,
Free from caring about
Other people's perceptions.
No longer your puppet
To alter and control,
Free from being an alter ego,
Free to be me, free to be whole.

Welcome to the reality of me,
The perfect balance of sexy and sweet,
Complete with all the beautiful imperfections,
Displayed in honor not for outside inspection.
Sensitive and loving so please be kind,
To my feelings, emotions and over-ambitious mind.
Successful in learning to be the best me,
All of the qualities acquired once I became free.

Free from your judgments,
Free from the misconceptions,
Free from caring about
Other people's perceptions.
No longer your puppet
To alter and control,
Free from being an alter ego,
Free to be me, free to be whole.

Universal Reversal

Survival for me
Was never guaranteed.
You see,
Cancer kept beating me, and beating me, and beating me
Into submission.
It's a condition known as decomposition
And by definition
I was supposed to just sit back and accept it
As in crept in
To my body and staked its claim
On my petite frame
And proclaimed victory
On a name
That did not belong to a VICTIM of cancer.
The answer is Sabrina
The question is "Who will survive?"
My inner drive
Competing with this disease
On my knees screaming "PLEASE...
IT'S...NOT...MY...TIME!!!"
And slowly...I open my eyes
And my demise
Is suddenly so far in the distance
That its existence
No longer exists.
I created a universal
Reversal
You see
Because cancer is now a victim of me.

Empty Prayers

Every night I prayed…
"If I should die before I wake,
I pray the Lord my soul to take…"
But it wasn't that easy
He wanted reasons
And explanations
For giving into sinful temptations
Here sat my salvation
Across from me
Drinking tea
At a marble table
And me, unable
To believe this encounter
And I hate to be a downer
But if you think for a second
That a second chance is promised, I reckon
You go home and do more than pray.
Go home and figure out a way
To correct the disarray
That you have caused
Go home and ponder on the image that you portray
The messages you convey.
Go home and rehearse the answers
On why He should rescue you from the demise of cancer.
I wasn't prepared
So I sat speechless and stared
Down upon my own body
Being revived by shoddy
Paddles
In disbelief that those doctors assumed they were in control.
It was at that moment when I handed over my soul
And promised to educate through this dream
Of writing which I have seen
Since I was just a little girl
With curls
Writing in bed
That roses are red

*In hopes that one day those roses would bloom
Into Lilies and Iris's filling the room.
I write for the dream
I write for that Supreme
Blessing to get my second chance
I write in hopes to never catch a glance
Of Him drinking tea at a marble table again.*

Butterflies

Seldom do we see beautiful butterflies
Glide
Into our lives
And land in the perfect location,
Enabling mere syllables like kindness, respect, & loyalty
To embrace personification
And become living beings,
Far beyond the scope of ones imagination, guaranteeing
A domain for us to thrive
And contrive
A world capable of inhabiting only beautiful butterflies,
Free from the rose thorns
And scorn
That we seem to encounter far too often,
These butterflies soften
The concrete and create a resplendent garden,
Transforming jargon
Into prose,
Never expecting gratitude from those
Lives that they brighten,
Merely hoping to enlighten
Those of us with the persistence
To constantly appreciate their existence.

My Diet is Messing with My Poetry

Splashing in pools of cheese sauce
Being penetrated by scoops of Tostitos,
I attempted to perfect my backstroke.

The popping of chicken frying
Sounds like the eloquence of Ms. Angelou
Performing a private reading in my living room.

Unable to forget the fulfillment of empty calories
I grab my carrot sticks
And curse the day Bugs Bunny was born.

Lesson in Art

Sitting beside a man on the corner of 5th & 82nd
We discussed life
Neither knowing the chapters in each others history books
Just discussing life
Questioning our decisions and releasing all judgments
I sat, head lazily down, and stared at the worn pavement
Kicking small pebbles with my high heels
Glancing over at the bare tattered feet of a man I hardly knew
I handed him ½ of my seafood wrap
And with mouths impolitely full
We continued to discuss life
Oblivious to the looks of disgust and disapproval
We were getting from passer-by's in a rush
To the oh-so-important meetings with zero significance
I was glad I took this moment
To just stop.
He asked me if I believed in angels
Eyes filled with tears,
Brows raised in anticipation of my answer
Tapping his right 4-fingered hand on the curb in nervous anxiety
And though I wasn't sure if I believed my own response
I said yes.
Our discussion of life ended at that moment
I stared at the empty space next to me
On the corner of 5th and 82nd
And could still faintly see the imprints of my friends tattered feet
Within an old puddle of oil
The answers weren't in front of my face
Or behind me hanging on a wall at the Met Museum of Art
They sat next to me,
Discussing life
As the art of an angel at work.

Perfected Pen Publishing is now accepting manuscripts for children's books, education and motivational/self-help genres. For submission guidelines, please visit www.PerfectedPenPublishing.com.

Perfected Pen Freelance Writing specializes in business writing including press releases, website content, newsletters, grants, social media campaigns and so much more. We also offer a wide variety of marketing material such as business cards and flyers. Contact us at www.PerfectedPen.com for more information or to obtain a free rate quote.

*Author photos provided by Angela Tappen Photography.
*Interior photos provided by stock.xchng.